# Wandering Woman: Nebraska

## The Ultimate Road Trip: One Woman's Journey Across the United States by RV

# Julie Bettendorf

# Contents

# Introduction

*"Not all who wander are lost." JRR Tolkien*

*Are you sure?* I thought to myself, as I tried not to panic. I was a long way from anything familiar, but that was how it should be. I had driven thousands of miles on dusty, pothole-filled roads. It's often on the worst roads that you can discover something truly amazing.

My dusty CRV was parked beside me, containing one restless dog and a variety of snack bags, all empty by now. There were no buildings in sight, no cars or people or movement at all. Only the constant humming of the insects as they buzzed around my head.

I turned to my left – another straight road that trailed off into the distance. I glanced over to the right, then behind me – two more barely discernible roads stretched out into the abyss. I was in a four-way intersection with no signs, no sense of direction, and no sign of life for several miles. No cell service either. *Damn*, I thought. *I'm lost*.

*How did I get here?* I couldn't help but feel like this little intersection was a cruel metaphor for life. I began to daydream, imagining each road might transport me back to a different time, a different role in my life, and a different me.

If I took the road from whence I came, it could lead me all the way back to Oregon, back to my cheating third husband, back to a life of loneliness and solitude. There is no greater loneliness than being married to someone who isn't actually present in your life.

If I took the road to my left, perhaps it could take me back to my career as a dental hygienist, a job I hated deep down in my soul. There is something so disengaging about cleaning teeth for a living. It's a disgusting, smelly way to get a paycheck. It pays well, which is great, but the best part is the huge gob of friends I enjoy to this day.

Or maybe the road to my right, *yes – maybe that's the path*, I imagined. Maybe it could take me back to my real treasure, my kids. Back to their smiling, innocent faces as toddlers, as they danced around the Christmas tree and their father and I were still married. Back when they still needed me for every little thing.

But, that was just it. I didn't feel needed anymore. My kids weren't toddlers anymore – they were both full-grown adults, and far too busy for me. My dental buddies were still working, but I wasn't. Dental hygiene had robbed me of the cartilage in my fingers, giving me severe, disabling arthritis. And, I wouldn't be returning to any more husbands either, because three marriages were quite enough for me.

All three of these paths, all three of these roles – the wife, the mother, and the dental hygienist – had seemingly been stripped from me within a year. I was lost and looking to find myself again.

The funny thing about this phrase, "not all who wander are lost" – is that, in my experience, wandering and being lost walk hand-in-hand with one another, and the expression can be flipped. In my experience, not all who are lost are wandering, and that is a real disservice to the beauty and clarity that the world has to offer.

When one becomes lost, wandering is the only option to guide oneself back to a path. After all, one could not come upon any dirt path at all without wandering.

I began wandering at an early age, both with my mind and with my feet. At eight years old, I was reading a book about archaeology and dreaming of one day seeing Egypt. I didn't follow a traditional path in high school either, going heavily into foreign languages, in hopes of one day using them.

At twenty-five years old, I divorced my first husband (the dental student who talked me into becoming a dental hygienist so I could work for him) and decided to give traveling a real shot. I took off for the Andes and Macchu Picchu, climbing up ancient Inca stone steps to reach the magnificent ruins.

Anyone who has been to Macchu Picchu will tell you there is something ethereal and deeply spiritual about the place. The ruins stretch out across the emerald green mountains, way up in the middle of the sky. Macchu Picchu gave me my first experience of feeling history. This trip inspired me to come back and complete a degree in archaeology, and I've been wandering ever since.

More travel followed including a backpack trip around Europe for three months, by myself, and trips to Britain, Italy, and Greece. I visited the burial places of Crusaders, mummies, and ancient kings. I happened upon the castle of my namesake in Bettendorf, Luxembourg, and wandered my way through European history.

My favorite excursion by far was finally seeing Egypt with my daughter in 2012. Just like my childhood dream envisioned, I rode a camel beneath the pyramids of Giza, with my head wrapped in some man's sweaty turban. It was perfect.

Traveling has always been my own personal antidote to pain. I went to Mexico after my first and second divorces, Canada after my third, and Italy after my dad died. Call it avoidance if you want, but I call it an accelerated form of healing in the purest sense of the word. I believe travel can heal your soul.

Wandering has always worked its wonders on me – made me feel renewed, rejoiceful, grateful, and purposeful. It's been my medicine.

So, as I stood in that intersection, I once again wondered how wandering had led me so astray this time. *What the hell am I supposed to do now?* It was then that I realized that one last path had not been considered yet – the path which stretched straight out in front of me. *Which role does this represent?* I pondered.

The answer smacked me in the face.

That last dirt road – the only path that could take me where I wanted to go, the only path that ever truly healed me or showed me the way – was the path of the traveler. The wife, the mother, and the hygienist roles – though valued in their time – were sitting in the bleachers now. It was time to welcome and enable my boldest, bravest, and perhaps most pivotal role yet:

The role of the Wandering Woman.

# Why You Need to Take a Road Trip

*A**merica, the beautiful?** I sure think so, but I didn't realize just how beautiful our country is until I embarked on traveling across the United States, full time, in a small RV.

The United States offers something for everyone. From spectacular beaches, austere mountains, to rolling plains, our country has it all. It's difficult to comprehend just how large and impressive our scenery is, until you experience it first-hand, with the ultimate road trip.

I also realized just how much of our history is missing from U.S. history I was taught as a kid. The history of our country didn't begin with the pilgrims landing on Plymouth Rock in the 1600s. Our history is far more ancient, with rock art and archaeological sites dating back over 12,000 years.

We owe a tremendous debt to early pioneers who tamed our land. The Mormons and other groups ventured into the great unknown with their families and their worldly possessions. Some of them pulled cumbersome handcarts across the country to settle in inhospitable, dangerous locations.

The goal of **Wandering Woman** is to bring history back to life and make it interesting again. I am presenting some famous sites, and many little-known ones. You will take the road-less-traveled with me, while we explore ghost towns, rock art sites, archaeological sites, and museums, to discover the colorful tapestry that is our country.

I present some history, including dates, but my goal is to present more of the real-life stories of history, including ghost stories, profiles in history, voices from the past, and moments in time, to give you, the reader, a deeper understanding of the context of history.

This is by no means an exhaustive list of places to visit. In fact, I encourage you to discover America for yourself, as I am doing, by making a trek across the land by car or RV. You can venture forth as the early explorers did, just a little more comfortably, with a lot less hardship.

I hope you enjoy this book and take a little time out to discover our beautiful country, and maybe even discover yourself in the process.

Safe Travels,

*Julie Bettendorf*

# Welcome to Wandering Woman

This book is for you – the grieving empty nester mom, the begrudged housewife, the woman in need of a drastic change in her life. Really, this book is for anyone with a passion for traveling. If you feel lost with no sense of direction or purpose in life, that's a bonus – this book will be even more appealing to you. And lastly, if you're a man reading this book, congratulations for holding a book with the word woman in the title. You're contributing to gender equality, and that's pretty neat.

I decided to combine three of my dearest loves – travel, history, and archaeology – and put them into a book because I believe wandering has the power to change your life. I have been to many areas of the world and have enjoyed too many outstanding experiences to list. However, by the time both my children moved out in 2017, I realized I was a stranger in my own country. It was the perfect time to explore a new country (my own) and discover a new me at the same time. I have been traveling for five years now, and I've upgraded to a small RV. I also have a new traveling companion, another sweet Sheltie, named Rosie. **Wandering Woman** is the chronicle of my journey across the United States, discovering the joy of getting lost and finding myself along the way.

# Welcome to Nebraska

## The Cornhusker State

*Nebraska* is one of the states that feeds us all. It's also gorgeous and green, with many historic sites to see. Pioneers crossed Nebraska, leaving their mark behind for history buffs like me. Many pioneers stayed in Nebraska, settling in to spend their lives in this great state. People are warm and friendly here, inviting you to return and enjoy their beautiful state.

## *5 Things to Love about Nebraska:*

- The green fields as far as the eye can see

- The famous military forts like Fort Robinson

- Early pioneer sites like Ash Hollow

- Wonderful museums like Harold Warp's Pioneer Village

- Spectacular rock formations like Chimney Rock

# Dreams of
# Nebraska

"We were at sea-there is no other adequate expression-on the plains of Nebraska." **Robert Louis Stevenson, on crossing the continent to California, August 23, 1879.**

"Anyone who spends time on the road knows there's something special about being in the middle of Utah or Nebraska - you sit with it, and there's a peace about it. You can go left or right, and it opens up all kinds of doors. You take your own path." **Jason Momoa**

"My great-grandmother grew up in a sod house in Nebraska. When she was a tiny girl - in other words, only four human generations ago - there were still enough wild bison on the Plains that she was *afraid lightning storms would spook them and they would trample her home."* **Derrick Jensen**

# Early Nebraska

**Early Transportation in Nebraska**

**Early Nebraska Homesteaders**

**Early Fort Robinson**

# Famous Nebraska Citizens

Crazy Horse, Oglala Sioux Warrior (1838–1877)

Fred Astaire, dancer and actor (1899–1987)

Marlon Brando, actor (1924–2004)

Henry Fonda, actor (1905–1982)

Warren Buffett, investor (1930-present)

Willa Cather, author (1873–1947)

Johnny Carson, entertainer  (1925–2005)

Malcolm X, human rights activist (1925–1965)

Gerald Ford, 38th President of the United States (1913–2006)

Buffalo Bill Cody, frontiersman and showman (1845–1917)

# Western Nebraska

# Fort Robinson

*F**ort Robinson* holds an important place in history. It's the location where the Cheyenne rebellion broke out in 1879. It's also the place where Sioux Chief Crazy Horse died. The fort is named to honor Lt. Levi Robinson who was killed by Indians while he was gathering wood.

The fort functioned as a military post from 1874 to 1948 and had several famous people stay there. Among the residents were Crazy Horse, Walter Reed, Red Cloud, Dull Knife,  and General Crook.

Crazy Horse gave himself up to authorities on September 5. He was taken to the guardhouse at Fort Robinson.

Crazy Horse escaped out the door of the guardhouse and was stabbed with a bayonet by the guard outside. He was taken to the adjutant's office where the fort surgeon tended to him. Crazy Horse died a few hours later.

Today you can see the officers' row, with residences built in 1874 to 1875. The adobe brick walls make them the oldest original buildings at Fort Robinson.

My favorite building is the Veterinary Hospital where the cavalry horses were cared for. There is also a 105 foot high flagstaff, complete with a ladder and crow's nest where the bugler would play.

You can visit the cemetery, with the first recorded burial being that of James Brogan, in 1875. The last burial was Fred Lester, in 1945. 258 people are buried in the cemetery.

### *How to get to Fort Robinson:*

Fort Robinson is located 3 miles west of Crawford on Hwy. 20

## *A moment in time: the Death of Crazy Horse*

Crazy Horse and 889 of his people surrendered to authorities at the Red Cloud Agency on May 6, 1877. Rumors began to spread that Crazy Horse was planning to escape and renew attacks on the whites. On September 3, General Crook ordered the arrest of Crazy Horse. Crazy Horse gave himself up to authorities on September 5. He was taken to the guardhouse at Fort Robinson.

Crazy Horse escaped out the door of the guardhouse and was stabbed with a bayonet by the guard outside. He was taken to the adjutant's office where the fort surgeon tended to him. Crazy Horse died a few hours later.

In January, 1879, Chief Dull Knife led the Cheyenne in a revolt against authorities because they lacked food, water, or heat during the winter. Soldiers went after the escaped Cheyenne, and massacred men, women, and children in what would become known as the Fort Robinson massacre.

## *Profiles in history:*

*Crazy Horse* was a Lakota Sioux warrior born in the 1840s near what is now Rapid City, South Dakota. He was known to be a brilliant tactician and fierce fighter and leader. Conflict began when prospectors and settlers came into the Black Hills, seeking gold. They crossed into reservation lands, violating the treaty the U.S. government had with the Lakota.

General Crook was tasked with managing the situation. Crazy Horse joined with the Cheyenne, waging war on Crook's troops, forcing their withdrawal. Crazy Horse then joined Sitting Bull to wage war at the Battle of the Little Bighorn in Montana. Crazy

Horse and his tribe suffered from starvation and cold, so Crazy Horse surrendered to General Crook at the Red Cloud Agency in Nebraska on  May 6, 1877. He was confined at Fort Robinson, and died there on September 5, 1877.

# Agate Fossil Beds

The ***Agate Fossil Beds*** is surrounded by stunning terrain. There is a trail that leads you past historic quarries where prehistoric mammal bones were found.

You can see spirals created by ancient beavers, known as Palaeocastors. The top of the spiral shows the ground level where the beavers lived.

### *How to get to Agate Fossil Beds:*

The Agate Fossil Beds are located at 301 River Road, 22 miles south of Harrison, Nebraska

# Scotts Bluff

**S** *cott's Bluff* was another important landmark for pioneers, settlers, and others traveling across the plains on the Oregon

Trail. It is a massive 800 foot tall sandstone and silt stone formation in the North Platte River Valley.

Native Americans referred to it as Meapate, which means "hill that is hard to go around."

Seven fur company employees were the first whites to visit the bluff, back in 1812. They were followed by other fur traders, including members of the Rocky Mountain Fur Company in 1828.

Legend has it that the company clerk, 23 year-old Hiram Scott, became ill during the trip, and was abandoned by his companions. He died near the bluff, and his remains were later found by the famous mountain man and guide, William Sublette in 1829. He was buried near the bluff which carries his name. Hill, NPS

In the town of Scotts Bluff, you can visit the grave of pioneer Rebecca Winters. She was the daughter of Gideon Burdick, a drummer boy in George Washington's army. Rebecca was born in New York in 1802, traveling to Utah as part of a Mormon pioneer group.

Rebecca became ill with cholera and died. A family friend carved the words "Rebecca Winters, age 50" on an iron wagon tire to mark her grave. Surveyors for the Burlington Railroad found the grave marker, and changed the path of the railroad, to protect the grave. In 1902, a permanent marker was erected.

## *How to get to Scotts Bluff:*

Scotts Bluff is located 3 miles west of the city of Gering.

## *Voices from the past:*

*"Scotts Bluffs are a perpetual monument to the tragedy of the death from starvation of a man of that name that was deserted by his companions on Laramie Fork, being too ill to travel, and the whole party without food. He lived to crawl 80 miles and leaves his bones in this place."* **Howard Egan, May 27, 1847.**

*"We traveled 15 miles and camped on the river, where the feed was poor and no wood. The bluffs on the other side of the river look like temples...this is a very curious looking place. The bluffs look like ancient edifices..."* **Patty Session, July 31, 1847.**

## *My story:*

Near Scotts Bluff is an area known as Robidoux Pass, named after Joseph E. Robidoux, the eldest son of the founder of St. Joseph, Missouri, Joseph Robidoux.  Joseph E. Robidoux is believed to be the guide for the American Fur Company, which came into the Scotts Bluff area in 1830.

Robidoux Pass is part of the original Oregon/California trail, which provided a way through the Wildcat Hills. Fur traders began to use the pass in the 1820s and 1830s. The first immigrants to use the pass were part of the Bidwell-Bartleson party in 1841.

A trading post was established by Antoine Robidoux in the 1850s. I drove the Robidoux Pass in search of the trading post, which according to the information I had, was still standing. The 13 miles is on a dirt road, with very little gravel, and lots of dust. Unfortunately, I left my back window open for my dog to get some air. After the trip, I looked back to discover a layer of dust over every surface of my van interior, including my dog's face. I looked everywhere for the phantom trading post, and after asking a researcher, discovered that the trading post is no longer in existence. It was dismantled 2 years ago. A sad end to a small piece of history.

## Ghost story:

The Scott's Bluff National Monument lies on the Oregon Trail. It is estimated that as many as 15,000 people died along the Oregon Trail, and very few of the graves are marked. The ghost of a woman wearing white has been seen walking along the base of the bluff after midnight. Could this be the ghost of an early settler who never made it to her final destination?

# Legacy of the Plains Museum

*The Legacy of the Plains Museum* is located on the Oregon Trail. The museum is an impressive place, with many artifacts of pioneer life. My favorite pieces were the historical photographs of life on the Nebraska plains.

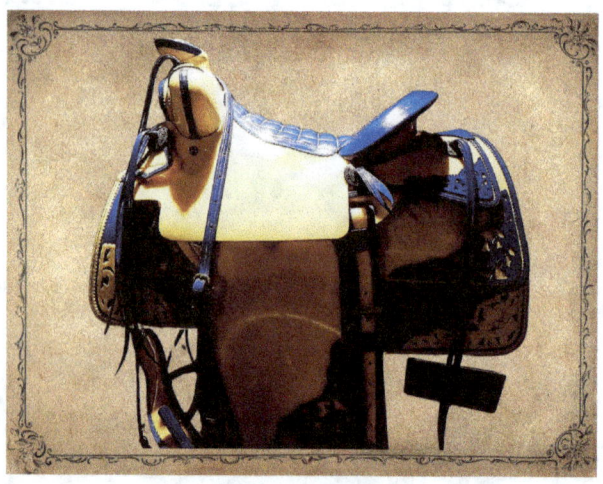

Another interesting piece is a saddle made of plastic. Each saddle was made by hand, so only 65 were ever produced.

There are extensive collections of Native American stone tools, projectile points. and artifacts.

One fascinating story retold in the museum is that of Bill and Mary Ann Hessler. While remodeling their garage, they discovered a wall of hand-hewn logs held together with square-headed nails. They also discovered a signature beam with the date 1887, the year Gering, Nebraska, was founded.

Originally, the Hessler's garage was a two room log cabin owned by pioneer merchant Frank Garlock and his wife, Nettie. Preservationists were able to preserve the room shown in the pictures above.

## *How to get to the Legacy of the Plains Museum:*

The Legacy of the Plains Museum is located at 2930 Old Oregon Trail in the town of Gering.

## *A Word about the Oregon Trail:*

The Oregon Trail travels across six states beginning with Missouri, then Kansas, Nebraska, Wyoming, Idaho, and finally, Oregon. Different branches of the Oregon Trail were used by groups of emigrants and came to be known as the California Trail and the Mormon Trail. The entire route was also known as the Overland Trail. Glassman

Between the years 1840 and 1866, approximately 500,000 pioneers traveled west on the trail. People died from diseases like scurvy, dysentery, and malaria. Many simply starved. Others suffered gunshot wounds.

It is believed that 34,000 to 45,000 people died along the trail, an average of between 17 and 22 lives per mile. Of the dead, only about 200 grave locations are known, most of which are unmarked. Many were intentionally buried in the path of the wagons, so any signs of a grave would not be noticed. Only about 20% of the Oregon Trail Ruts are identifiable today. [Wagner]

## *Voices from the past:*

*"Just threw my mirror way some while back. Why I couldn't bear the sight of my face no more, all over with creases and splotches. Looking so...so common. But my feet. Well, there is no escaping the*

*sight of my feet. I watch them step after step, mile after mile. Won't fit no proper shoes."* **Unknown Oregon Trail Pioneer.**

*"Honore Liberty Timfret, wife of Zabel Timfret, I am. Birthed four fine girls and a son, I did. But that's forever been taken from me. My Timothy and Elizabeth fell to cholera early on. Somehow my heart hardened to sustain me. It took me quite a spell, you can imagine, but most recently the sight of graves has gone almost unnoticed. I begged Zabel for some kind of marker to show my child's spot. "How will Jesus find them without a marker" But no amount of cajolin' or cryin' would change that man's mind. So, we buried them back there in the great nothing with nary a thing to mark the spot but the never-ending wind."* **HonoreTimfret, Oregon Trail Pioneer.**

# Chimney Rock

*C**himney Rock* is 600 miles from Independence, Missouri, the starting point on the Oregon Trail. It was first mentioned as a "chimney" in an 1827 report. It later became known as "Chimney Rock" by travelers along the Oregon Trail in the 1840s.

Chimney Rock could be seen as much as 30 miles away. It was a welcome first landmark for weary emigrants. The Chimney Rock Pony Express Station was once located between Chimney Rock and the North Platte River.

Chimney Rock is 325 feet tall and rises 470 feet above the North Platte River Valley.

## *How to get to Chimney Rock:*

Chimney Rock is located in Western Nebraska, near the town of Bayard

## *A moment in time: the Schoolchildren's Blizzard of 1888*

The day was a crisp January 12th in 1888. A ferocious blizzard swept down over the Midwest. It's called the Schoolchildren's Blizzard because so many children died in it, on their way home from school. What started out as a beautiful winter morning turned into a deadly torrent of ice crystals and wind, suffocating and freezing anyone unfortunate enough to be outside.

It's estimated between 250 and 500 people died in the blizzard. Many of the bodies were found days, weeks, and even months later, often in heartbreaking circumstances, including small groups of children and adults, trying to save each other.

"They were found standing waist deep in drifts with their hands frozen to barbed-wire fences, clutching at straw piles, buried under overturned wagons, on their backs, face down on the snow with their arms outstretched as if trying to crawl." [Laskin]

Nebraska has its share of victims of the blizzard, including Etta Shattuck, a teacher who sent her children home. They made it safely, but Etta didn't. She lost both her legs from frostbite and died a few days later. Two young sisters named Westphalen left school to return home and were found frozen in a field. The older sister had wrapped her coat around her younger sister, trying to save her. [Lee]

# Ash Hollow

*A**sh Hollow State Historical Park* is a beautiful spot of great importance in history. Windlass Hill, was a tortuous spot for emigrants traveling along the Oregon-California Trail.

Pioneers had a difficult time going down the 300 foot hill, which lies at a 25 degree angle, and had to lower their wagons by ropes. Wagon ruts can still be seen on the hill.

There is a stone school, built in 1903, and the site of an early mail station, built in 1854. The mail station was destroyed by a group of Sioux Indians in 1855. The school remained open until 1919.

In the Ash Hollow Cemetery nearby, you can visit the grave of Rachel E. Pattison, an early pioneer who died June 19, 1849. Rachel died of cholera while trying to reach the Oregon Territory from Illinois. She was a recent bride of two months, and was just 18 years old.

### *How to get to Ash Hollow:*

Ash Hollow State Historical Park is 5 miles south of the town of Lewellen.

## *A word about cholera:*

Cholera is caused by ingesting food or water contaminated by Vibrio cholerae bacteria. The disease can be deadly, causing diarrhea, vomiting, dehydration, and eventually, death. Cholera risk is minimal in modern times due to clean water and food, and medical treatment. For the pioneers, it was deadly. The years 1849, 1850, and 1852 were the worst for cholera breakouts along the Oregon Trail. Some groups lost up to two-thirds of their party. The emigrants medical solution was to ingest a mixture of cornmeal and whiskey. [Hill]

# Gothenburg Pony Express Station

The **Pony Express Station** which now sits in Ehmen Park in Gothenburg, Nebraska, was built on the Oregon Trail in 1854. The house was originally used as a trading post for fur trappers, and then as a ranch house. It became a Pony Express Station in 1860, and was used by Pony Express Riders until the Pony Express ended in 1861.

The building then became a stage station for the Overland Trail, followed by a bunkhouse, storage area, and then a residence until 1931, when it was donated to the city of Gothenburg.

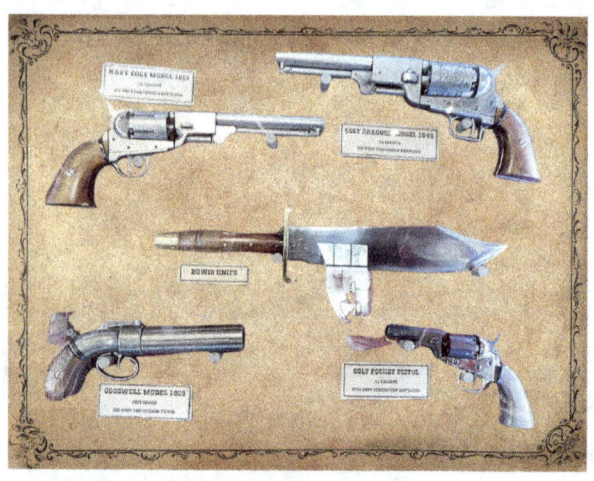

The station contains a small museum with a Pony Express mochila, which was a pouch to carry the mail, and a collection of weapons carried by the Pony Express riders.

### *How to get to the Gothenburg Pony Express Station:*

The Gothenburg Pony Express Station is located at 510 15th St, Gothenburg, Nebraska

## Voices from the past:

*"Wanted, young, skinny, wiry fellows not over eighteen. Must be expert riders, willing to risk death daily. Orphans preferred. Wages $25 a week"* **job posting from a San Francisco newspaper, March 1860.** Corbett

*"Greatest of all inventions to me, because it affected me directly, is the telegraph. In the two minutes we used to be allowed to change horses at a station, Western Union now sends a message to New York or even London, The telegraph today does in a second what it took eighty young men and hundreds of horses eight days to do when I was a rider in the Pony Express."* **William Campbell, pony express rider, at age 94.** Corbett

## Fun facts about the Pony Express:

- The Pony Express ran from 1860 to 1861 and was replaced by the telegraph

- The route ran from St. Joseph, Missouri to Sacramento, California, a distance of 1900 miles

- Highway 50, known as the "loneliest road in America" was part of the mail route from Sacramento to Salt Lake City in 1851.

- There were 190 stations along the route, when the Pony Express was in peak operation

- Each station was equipped with 2 agents, 1 station keeper, and 1 assistant

- There were 420 horses used at peak times, along with 80 riders

John Fisher, John Hancock, and Billy Fisher, Pony Express Riders

- Pony Express riders weighed an average of 100 to 120 pounds, and their average age was 19

- Horses were usually half-wild mustangs, famous for their speed and the fact that they never got tired

- They rode an average speed of 7 miles per hour, which meant that it took them an average of 10 days to complete the trip

- Each rider rode 60 to 120 miles before changing riders

- The fastest ride ever was 7.5 days to deliver Abraham Lincoln's Inaugural address

- William C. "Buffalo Bill" Cody rode 322 miles in 21 hours and 40 minutes using 21 horses

- Riders were paid $120 to $125 per month

- A letter cost $5 in gold, paid in advance[Corbett]

# Eastern Nebraska

# Fort Hartsuff

***F****ort Hartsuff* was active as a military post from 1874 to 1881 and was named after General George Hartsuff, a Civil War hero.

The fort protected settlers and served as a separation between Pawnee and Sioux tribes, who were mortal enemies.

In the 1870s, soldiers at the fort created a new trail to the gold fields of the Black Hills in South Dakota.

The main buildings are built of a durable lime and concrete mixture, preserving them against fierce Nebraska winters.

The hospital is an interesting building. It appears small on the outside, but is full of hospital beds and has a comfortable sitting area on the inside.

Don't miss the bone saw, a formidable tool used for amputations. There is also an interesting exhibit about trephination, which involved cutting a hole in the skull to relieve pressure.

The duplex building housed officers and their families. In an 1880 census, 14 people lived here.

The inside furnishings are comfortable, with fireplaces, and pi-
anos.

You can also visit the General Prison Room, where civilian prisoners and deserters were kept.

Other buildings to visit include the barracks building, commissary, and blacksmith buildings.

## *How to get to Fort Hartsuff:*

Fort Hartsuff is located at 82034 Fort Avenue in Burwell, Nebraska.

# Fort Kearny

***F**ort Kearny* began its life in 1848 and was the first post to be established to protect travelers on the Oregon-California Trail.

It was first known as Fort Childs, but was later renamed after General Stephen Watts Kearny.

The fort was used to carry messages for gold seekers heading west. It also was a Pony Express station and stage stop.

In 1864 through 1865 during the Indian Wars, a stockade was built around the fort to protect it. The fort was closed in 1871 and much of it was dismantled.

## *How to get to Fort Kearny:*

Fort Kearny is located at 1020 V. Road in Kearney, Nebraska

# Harold Warp's
# Pioneer Village

*Harold Warp's Pioneer Village* in Minden, Nebraska, is a one-of-a-kind experience, put together by a one-of-a-kind man with a vision, Harold Warp. Harold Warp began his vision in 1948 and now his museum contains over 50,000 artifacts showing the progress man has made since 1830.

Outside, there are 28 buildings including a log cabin and stockade built in 1869 which was used as a fort. Five families lived within the stockade.

Other buildings include a Pony Express Station and barn, which were part of the Deadwood Trail during and after the Black Hills Gold Rush of 1876.

The little limestone building is the Land Office, and was built in 1874. It's where Nebraska homesteaders first filed their claims for land.

There is also America's oldest merry-go-round at the site.

One of my favorite individual pieces outside is a beautiful foot tub and water pitcher from 1780,  made by Josiah Wedgewood. It was found in a Mississippi Plantation.

In addition to the buildings outside, there is a spectacular indoor museum full of everything from old vehicles, to clocks, to furnishings.

One of my favorite pieces is the 1893 Sicilian cart, known as a carretta.

These carts were hand-painted with historical or religious-themed pictures, and were used to carry both people, and supplies.

There is also the Bowman Show Wagon, donated by Fay Bowman,
who was born in the cart in 1902. The wagon was built in 1899 by
Fay's father and was used as part of a traveling road show.

Another fabulous vehicle is a Gypsy Wagon from 1850.   There are only a few of these in existence, because when the owner of the wagon died, the wagon was burned along with the owner's personal belongings.

### *How to get to Harold Warp's Pioneer Village:*

Harold Warp's Pioneer Village is located at 138 E. Hwy. 6, in the town of Minden.

## *Profiles in history:*

*Harold Warp* was born in 1903, in a sod house on the Nebraska prairie, and was the youngest of 12 children. His parents died when he was 11, so he moved in with an older brother in the town of Minden.

He invented an inexpensive plastic to replace broken windows for farmers in the area. Warp applied for a patent, called the material Flex-O-Glass, and the rest is history. He also invented the first plastic garbage bag, and a polyethylene food wrap he called Jiffy Wrap.

He became a millionaire manufacturer of plastics by the time he was 50 years old. He used his wealth to acquire buildings from his childhood, including his one-room schoolhouse. Harold Warp died in 1994, at the age of 90, leaving behind his fabulous Pioneer Village.

## *Voices from the past:*

*"I saw all these things come. I saw the first automobiles. I remember when the preacher's son put together the first radio, I remember the first rural free delivery, the first graded road."* **Harold Warp, thoughts on progress**

# The Plainsman Museum

The *Plainsman Museum* is in the town of Aurora, and it has a little something for everyone, displaying 100 years of exploration and settlement of Hamilton County, Nebraska.

Inside the museum you can see a recreated village with shops and businesses, including a glassworks shop, leather goods, a general store, a doctor's office, a dentist's office, and more.

This money chest, from around 1870, is one of my favorite pieces. It held $40,000 in gold ($803,200) today, and was to be used for purchasing land,

Each of the buildings contains historic artifacts which look as though they might have been left there yesterday.

There are entire buildings within the museum, including a log cabin from the 1850s.

Log cabins were a rare sight on the Great Plains, because lumber was scarce.

A much more common sight was a sod house, known as a "soddy."

Outside the museum, you can visit a beautiful Victorian residence known as the Bates House, built in 1876, by Civil War veteran of the Union army, General Delevan Bates.

### How to get to the Plainsman Museum:

The Plainsman Museum is located at 210 16th St, in Aurora, Nebraska

# Homestead
# National
# Monument

*T*he *Homestead National Monument* is a wonderful indoor/outdoor museum, full of artifacts that celebrate the Homestead Act of 1862. When you walk the grounds of the Homestead National Monument, you will come upon a cabin built by George W. Palmer in 1867. He cut the wood for the cabin walls and formed the bricks himself by hand.

He and his wife, and their five children lived in the cabin. Eventually, the Palmers had five more children, so the cabin housed a family of twelve .

Another building close by is the Freeman School, built of bricks in 1872. The bricks were made by Thomas Freeman, a local landowner. Daniel Freeman, who was no relation to Thomas, taught at the school. The first day of school, 14 students attended.

An interesting story associated with the Freeman School concerns an incident which happened in 1899. Edith Beecher, a teacher at the school, read Bible verses, sang hymns, and prayed with the schoolchildren.

Daniel Freeman asked the school board, and later the district court, to stop Beecher. They refused. Freeman appealed to the Nebraska Supreme Court, who ruled that Beecher's actions were religious worship, and did not belong in a public school.

### *How to get to the Homestead National Monument:*

The Homestead National Monument is located at 8523 West State Hwy. 4 close to the town of Beatrice.

## *A word about the Homestead Act:*

The Homestead Act was passed by Congress and signed into Law by Abraham Lincoln in 1862. The act granted 160 acres each to pioneers who promised to live on the acreage for at least 5 years. In that time, the land owner promised to build a house, dig a well, fence the land, plow 10 acres, and live on the property. All comers were eligible, as long as the filing fee of $18 was paid. Laskin

## *Voices from the past:*

*"There seemed to be nothing to see; no fences, no creeks or trees, no hills or fields... There was nothing but land: not a country at all, but the material out of which countries are made."* **Willa Cather, 1918**

## *My story:*

When I drove out to the Freeman School to photograph it, I parked my RV on what I thought was a shoulder. I opened the side door and took a step out, only to find I was dangling in space. I clung to the door handle, pulling the door completely off its hinges to save myself from falling into a ravine. My camera was wrapped precariously around my neck. I managed to sprain my ankle, and bruise my body and my ego. I ended up using a bungee cord to secure the door until I could get it fixed. I managed some nice photos of the school though.

Travel tip: when in the Midwest, note that wide shoulders to park on are not as wide as you think, or they are completely non-existent.

# Rock Creek Station

***R****ock Creek Station* is historic and wonderful. The area of Rock Creek was first explored by John C. Fremont and Kit Carson.

These two explorers carved their names on a sandstone bluff in 1842, but the signatures are no longer visible. A large boulder containing a metal plaque in front of the museum commemorates their arrival.

The first Rock Creek Station was built in 1857 by S.C. Glenn and Newton Glenn to serve people traveling along the Little Blue River. The Glenns built a store, a barn, and living quarters. The Glenns sold the station in 1859 to David McCanles.

McCanles built a new station with a better water supply on the east side of the river. He built a cabin, stable, corrals, and a station containing a store. McCanles also built a toll bridge in 1859, for travelers with wagons to cross the steep bank.

Throughout the grounds you can see deep trail ruts carved by travelers' wagons on the Oregon and California Trails.

You can also see three grave markers, which are some of the few pioneer grave markers which still exist along the historic trails. The names have long since worn away.

The stone post office is a replica of the original built on the site in 1865.

The West Ranch Cabin sold provisions to travelers along the trail.

Typical prices of goods at the Rock Creek Station in the 1860s were:

- Whiskey 15-25 cents per drink

- Tobacco $1.00

- Flour $12-$15 per hundred weight

- Salt Pork 30-40 cents per pound

- Coffee 60-75 cents per pound

- Tea $2.00-$3.00 per pound

The toll bridge was built in 1859 by David McCanles and was used by travelers to cross a steep, rocky ravine.

McCanles charged between 10 cents and 1.50, according to the weight of the wagon, and how much they could afford to pay.

The East Ranch portion of the park contains replicas of the Pony Express barn and the bunk house, where travelers stayed, including Mark Twain, who stayed at the Rock Creek Station on his way to Nevada.

The East Ranch Cabin is a famous spot in history. It is where Wild Bill Hickok first earned his reputation as a gunfighter. Wild Bill killed David McCanles there on July 12,1861.

The Rock Creek Station museum has many interesting artifacts, including this ornate powder flask.

Two of my favorite pieces are these clay pipes.

## *How to get to Rock Creek Station:*

Rock Creek Station is located at 57426 710th Rd, Fairbury, NE, in the Southeastern part of the state.

## *A moment in time: Hickok kills McCanles, July 12, 1861*

McCanles sold out to the Overland Stage Company and Pony Express, who were to pay McCanles on a payment plan. The company sent caretakers named Wellman, who had a 23-year-old stock tender named James Hickok. McCanles was expecting his final payment on the sale of the property, and he went to seek payment from the Wellmans. McCanles son, Monroe, went with him.

McCanles came face to face with Hickok, who grabbed a rifle and shot McCanles through the heart. The date was July 12, 1861. Hickok, Wellman, and another stock tender named Brink were arrested and tried in Beatrice, Nebraska. They were found to have committed the shooting in self-defense, because McCanles, justified or not, had confronted Wellman and Hickok, and McCanles was a powerfully built man with a hot-tempered reputation.

### Voices from the past:

*"We three were the only passengers, this trip. We sat on the back seat, inside. About all the rest of the coach was full of mail bags-for we had three days delayed mail with us. Almost touching our knees, a perpendicular wall of mail matter rose up to the roof. There was a great pile of it strapped on top of the stage, and both the fore and hind boots were full. We had twenty-seven hundred pounds of it aboard..."* **Samuel Clemens (Mark Twain) traveling through Rock Creek Station on his way to Carson City, Nevada, 1861.**

# Indian Cave State Park

*Indian Cave State Park* is located within what is known as the "Nebraska Ozarks" a heavily forested area of immense beauty, bordering the Missouri River. Lewis and Clark came into the area in 1804. The park is named for a large sandstone cave, the use of which dates back thousands of years.

The cave contains ancient petroglyphs, which are believed to have been carved 1,500 to 1,800 years ago. Overgrown brush and extreme wear make them difficult to see. The date and artists are not known.

The state park contains what remains of St. Deroin, which began its life in 1853, as one of the first areas of settlement in Nebraska territory. The town was named for Joseph Deroin, a trader who owned the land. The "Saint" was added to the name to create an image of a larger city, like St. Louis. The town reached a total of 300 people in the 1870s, before beginning a slow slide into ghost town status.

As you walk around St. Deroin, you can see a restored mercantile building, and an original brick schoolhouse, complete with original desks and woodstove. Don't miss the framed flag on the wall, containing 46 stars.

You can also visit the St. Deroin cemetery, where the early residents of St. Deroin are spending eternity. The first burial was that of Joseph Deroin himself, buried in 1858.

## How to get to Indian Cave State Park:

Indian Cave State Park is located 10 miles south of Brownville and 5 miles east on S-64E.

## *Profiles in history:*

Joseph DeRoin was born in 1819 near Bellevue, Nebraska. His father was a Metis trader and his mother was an Otoe Indian. Joseph set up a trading post in the main village of Otoes. Joseph had three wives and at least nine children. He was killed while trying to collect a six dollar debt owed to him and is buried in the St. Deroin cemetery. According to a legend, he was buried with his horse, and the bridle and saddle were placed in the notch of a tree. The belief was that an Indian warrior would use his horse's spirit to ride into Heaven.

# Favorite Places to Camp

***Robidoux RV Park*** is the perfect home base to explore nearby areas including Gering, the Legacy of the Plains Museum, Scotts Bluff, and more. The campground is large, with spacious sites, and lots of green grass, trees, squirrels, and bunnies for you and your dog to enjoy. There are 42 spaces with picnic tables and full hook-ups. There is also a shower and laundry building. For more information and to make reservations, please visit ***https://www .campspot.com/book/robidoux-rv-park***

***Rock Creek Historical Park Campground*** has 25 well spaced camping sites with electrical hookups, basic campsites, and equestrian campsites. There are showers, restrooms, fire pits, and picnic tables. The grounds are peaceful, with several hiking and horse trails. For more information, please visit ***OutdoorNebras ka.gov***

***Indian Cave State Park*** is an excellent location to explore Southeastern Nebraska. The state park has 2 campgrounds with a total of 134 camping sites, half of which are reservable, and half are a first come, first served basis. Most are electric, with fire pits and picnic tables. There are showers and flush toilets within the park. Enjoy the many hiking trails and expansive views. For more information, visit ***OutdoorNebraska.gov.***

# Travel Tips & Stuff

## What You Need to Know

### *How to get started:*

P lanning your trip should be one of the most exciting things about it. You want to be spontaneous, but it is also very wise to plan your route, so you can take full advantage of all the time and miles you will invest.

- First, decide your passions. If you love airplanes, trains, or old vehicles, plan your trip around that. If you love gardens or architecture, seek that out as the focus of your trip.

- Next, read and research areas of the country that will let you enjoy what you are interested in.

- Make a list by state and city or town, of what you want to see.

- Take your handy road atlas and locate the areas on the pages.

- Make a tentative route plan, so you have an idea of where you are going.

***Travel tip:*** Avoid trying to plan your trip down to a schedule of days, hours, or minutes. On a road trip, it will be virtually impossible to know where you will be on any given day. If you adhere to a schedule, you are more likely to stress out, and less likely to actually enjoy yourself, which is the whole point.

## What you need:

You need to bring along a sense of adventure and a curious mind. You need to ditch the idea of always being on a schedule, and live a little more spontaneously to thoroughly enjoy yourself. Things will happen as you travel, both good things and bad things, and you need to prepare your mind and your soul for day-to-day changes.

So much of our lives are planned out. Between growing up, going to school, finding a career, marriage, kids, or whatever,  people have lost much of the ability to be spontaneous. But you must take spontaneity on the trip with you, because you may make detours along the way to see something really spectacular.

### So, for the practical stuff you need:

***A great vehicle***-I am now five years into the trip and have swapped out my Honda CRV for a small RV, just under 20 feet. I go small because I see humongous RVs on the road, towing a car behind, and all I can think of is, they can't go just anywhere. They are too big. Bad gas mileage, cumbersome to drive, slow, and not agile like my small RV. So, I encourage you, if you want to go car or RV camping and be able to go on remote dirt roads, get an agile vehicle, and small RVs are great.

***Travel tip:*** Don't be afraid to do some modifications to your vehicle. I have made many alterations to my RV, including changing the plumbing, which used to be a mere 4 inches off of the ground, so I would break it all the time. It's now encased in my outside storage compartment. I am also a minimalist, so I have jettisoned anything I won't use or don't love. Don't be afraid to get rid of unnecessary stuff.

***An awesome camera*** that you know inside and out. I use a Nikon and it takes wonderful pictures. Don't skimp on a camera, and don't think a cellphone camera is all you need, because you want the best for your beautiful photos.

***Window shades***-the best ones are magnetic so you just place them against your windows and they cling to them, obscuring the view inside your car. I also have magnetic window screens, so I can leave my windows down with no bugs!

***Battery operated fans and lights***-these are important, so you don't have to rely on your house batteries for light and cooling options.

***Portable air compressor***-this little gem plugs into your cigarette lighter and will inflate your tires if you have a flat. Make sure the air compressor can reach to all of your tires, including your rear tires.

***Portable battery charger and power bank***-mine comes with battery cables and the power bank, yet once inside the case, it is small enough to put in your glove compartment. This little item, unfortunately, I have had to use, and it saved me.

***Portable generator***-I have two gas powered generators on the back of my RV, which are hooked together with a coupling unit. I have an interior generator, but after much expense and multiple repairs, it still doesn't work. Now I have generators which will run everything, including AC, and I can maintain them myself.

***All season clothing***-you never know what different states will bring for weather, so take hot weather and cold weather clothes, and a fair amount of shoes appropriate for hiking, or walking, sandals, and slippers, which are nice at night. Also take along a pair of cheap rubber flip-flops to wear in the public showers you might go into.

***Your own pillows***-I like my own pillows, so I don't wake up with neck cramps, especially after sleeping in the car.

***Sleeping bag and cozy blankets***-you want to stay warm and layering is everything.

***Warm hat, warm socks, and fuzzy jammies*** to keep you warm for cold nights sleeping in the car.

***A great road atlas***, and great guidebooks-get one that's easy to read, with great pictures. For a road atlas, just get one that is easy to read.

## *A word about photography:*

Along with a great camera, you need to have a great eye. This is easier than it sounds once you have worked with your camera and are comfortable taking pictures with it. I am not a professional photographer, but I like my pictures and other people do too.

These are my tips for taking great pictures:

- Experiment with taking both horizontal and vertical shots.

- Don't always put the subject of the photo in the middle of the photograph.

- This one is important: pay attention to the foreground, and if possible, have something, a plant or whatever, in the foreground to help give the photo dimension and depth.

- This one is important too: turn around often to see the view you just came from. I do this quite often and some of my best pictures have resulted from when I turned around and took the shot.

You can also take a mental photo. Place an image in your mind that you can call upon later. Use all of your senses to see, hear, smell, and maybe even to taste, what is around you. You have the means to fully experience your surroundings, and that is very important to a traveler. When you take a mental photo, be sure to jot down quick little details about what you saw, heard, smelled, or tasted, so you can jog your memory later.

And last, but not least...don't be posing in front of everything, everywhere, to show that you actually went somewhere. Most people want to see themselves in your photo and be mentally transported there, but they can't if you are there already.

## *To camp or not to camp:*

Car or RV camping is great. I prefer it to sleeping on the cold, hard ground in a tent. I can lock the doors, put my window shades up and be cozy for the night.

Some people camp in a Walmart parking lot and feel safe. I do not. I believe that if you are in a busy area, you are more likely to be confronted by a nut job who may bother you. Nothing against Walmart, and many Walmart stores don't allow overnight parking. I don't go for rest areas either because they have a track record of incidents happening to people in rest areas, especially women travelers.

I have come to love casino parking lots. I enjoy gambling, so for a little money, many casinos will provide overnight stays if you gamble a little inside the casino. I also do a lot of boondocking, because it's free, and I believe you are safer parked out in the middle of nowhere in the dark.

I also enjoy camping In state or national campgrounds, wildlife sanctuaries, and fairgrounds.

## *A word about safety:*

When you are a woman traveling alone, it's critical to keep a low profile. Don't tell people you are traveling alone, where you are staying, or any other personal information.

I don't go to bars or get drunk. I'm not preaching but you are on your own, in a city or town you've never been to, and you don't know anyone, so it's not the time to lose control of what you are doing. When you are in control, you are better able to decide which people you want to get to know better.

***Travel tip:***  If you feel vulnerable traveling alone, that's OK. Vulnerability is part of passion, and traveling is a passionate thing to do. You can put one of those family stickers on your vehicle to indicate to others that you are not traveling alone, which can help you feel more secure.

## *Maintain your connections:*

When you are traveling alone, there is a definite sense of discon-nection. It feels almost like you are the only one in the world, traveling through space and time. That's why it's critical to keep your connections to loved ones active.

Be on Facebook while you are traveling. You may not have internet a lot of the time, or the internet will be poor. Consider paying to have your phone be a hotspot. It's a little bit of money per month, but it's worth it and has saved me from being without internet. I love the convenience of it, and you will too.

Plan your journey around visiting family members or friends you haven't seen for a long time, or people that are good friends. When you see people you know, it will ground you, so you can continue traveling.

Check in by phone with loved ones. They worry about you, and it's good for both of you to stay connected no matter where you are.

Consider traveling with a pet. I now travel with my 12 year-old sheltie Rosie, after losing my beloved sheltie, Sadie. Rosie is a wonderful companion. She is also an excellent watchdog, and barks her head off at other dogs and people.

***Travel tip:*** One of the easiest and best ways I stay connected while traveling is to offer to take a photo for someone I don't know. Many couples, families, or singles would love to have more pictures of themselves traveling. It's an easy and quick way to have a connection with a fellow traveler, and it's good manners too.

## *Practical matters:*

You need to have an address to send your mail to. Keep in touch with whomever is nice enough to do this for you.

You will also need to come back occasionally to register your car, vote, go to doctor visits, and take care of any other business. You can't leave it all behind, as tempting as that may be.

## *Bad things that happened:*

I have had a few problems, mostly associated with my RV. I bought an older model, vintage 1999, and I have had to do a few repairs.

My worst experience came when I took my rig in to a shop in Spokane, Washington (who shall remain nameless.) All I needed was an oil change. I got the oil change and was about an hour south of town on a Friday at 4:30, when my engine blew.

I was in the middle of the eastern Washington prairie, many miles from the nearest town. All I could do was watch my oil drain out onto the Interstate. I can't help but think it was associated with my oil change, but I couldn't prove it. The moral of this story is: DON'T LET JUST ANYONE WORK ON YOUR VEHICLE.

### *Good things that happened:*

I have met many great people on my travels, from all walks of life. I have also learned not to judge people. I have met numerous homeless people who are often just wanting a kind word, and not to be treated like dirt.

People have mistaken me for a homeless person, and I too, have been treated like dirt. When I can, I try to help people and be kind to them. Most of the time, they smile and reciprocate. You will always meet people who are unkind, but they are just as likely to be driving a huge expensive rig, or to be homeless.

We are all Americans, and we are all part of the human race. When you meet people across the country, you realize just how important it is to get to know your fellow citizens, and learn more about how they view the world and our country.

I have to give a special shout-out to the many dedicated people, often volunteers, who staff our state and national parks and monuments. They work tirelessly to ensure the health of our natural resources, and help travelers enjoy their visit. The same is true of the many people who staff the museums in small towns and large cities. They enjoy history, like I do, and it shows in their smiles.

Along with wonderful people, I have seen an America that is spectacularly beautiful, with open prairies, majestic mountains, and crystal clear rivers. I have seen a small fraction of the history of our country. I have seen the memorials to the brave people who shaped our country. I have fallen in love with America in a way that was not possible sitting in my living room. People ask me, "would I do it again?" The answer comes easily, "Yes, in a heartbeat."

# Random Thoughts
## What History Means to Me

F irst, let me start by sharing with you my opinion of what history isn't. History is not a collection of random dates, names, and places for you to memorize. History is not a dry and uninteresting class you have to pass to graduate.

I believe history is a tangible thing. You can actually *feel* history in the places you go, and the sights you see. I remember walking up to the Acropolis in Athens. I looked down at the well-worn marble steps and wondered about how many ancient philosophers had climbed these very steps, thousands of years ago.

You don't have to go far away to experience the *feeling* of history. If you are lucky enough to live in an old house, you may experience history in your own surroundings. You might say to yourself, *"If only these walls could talk."*

During my travels across the United States, I *felt* history in many, many places. If you travel across the country like I did, you will *feel* the wonderful history of our beautiful country for yourself, and you will never be the same. You will discover what it means to be an American.

## *Why I travel, and why you should too:*

I decided to travel across the country by car because I wanted to rediscover America. When I first set out to explore the history of our country, I wanted to find out why America is the greatest country on earth, and what it means to be an American.

The politics of these United States can be frightening and polarizing. I prefer to focus on what unites us, not what divides us. What unites us is we all live in a spectacularly beautiful country, with warm, wonderful people.

I began my journey five years ago, starting out in my Honda CRV. I soon realized I loved the lifestyle, so now I travel in a small RV. From my small RV, I look out on a country with a unique and colorful, multicultural tapestry, unlike any other country on earth.

I have a degree in Archaeology, and a passion for all things archaeological. I love history, with a side love of paleontology. It is these three passions that I set my trip agenda around. I set out to discover the archaeological sites, history, and paleontological world of our country.

As I travel and write my books, I get asked all the time, especially by women, "What is it like to travel by yourself? Aren't you scared?" The truth is, I believe everyone should do what I did. It's a wonderful way to discover our country, and to rediscover yourself. The truth is, I'm scared not to travel. Traveling allows you to get to know yourself, in ways not possible when sitting on the couch watching TV.

We tend to spend a lot of our lives tuning out the world and our place within it. When you travel, you are quite literally forced to deal with your own thoughts, emotions, and feelings. You can discover yourself while traveling. You can come to understand what makes you who you are, and how you can perhaps become a better person. Above all, traveling gives you mental clarity to figure out how to live with intent. It's a way to guide your life, not just wait for things to happen.

# Bibliography & Further Reading

Carey, John. *Eyewitness to History*, Harvard University Press, 2003

Corbett, Christopher. *Orphans Preferred: the Twisted Truth and Lasting Legend of the Pony Express*. Broadway Books, 2004

Destination Western Nebraska, Nebraska Travel and Tourism, 2023

Enss, Chris. *Tales behind the Tombstones*. Morris Pub., 2007

Finch, etc. al.., Jackie. *Eyewitness Travel USA*. DK Publishing, 2017

Fort Hartsuff State Historical Park, Outdoor Nebraska, 2017

Fort Robinson State Park, Outdoor Nebraska 2023

Glassman, Steve. *It Happened on the Santa Fe Trail*. Twodot, 2008

Hill, William E. *The Oregon Trail, Yesterday and Today: a Brief History and Pictorial Journey along the Wagon Tracks of Pioneers*. Caxton Press, 2014

Indian Cave State Park, Outdoor Nebraska 2023

Johnson, Mary E. Benson. *Reminiscences of Oregon Pioneers*. East Oregonian Pub. Co., 1937

Jones, Landon Y. *The Essential Lewis and Clark*. Harper Collins Publishers, 2000

Laskin, David, *The Children's Blizzard.* Harper Collins Publishers, 2004

Lee, Wayne C. *Bad Men & Bad Towns*, Caxton Press, 2010

*Lewis and Clark National and State Historical Parks*, National Park Service

Nebraska State Parks Guide, Outdoor Nebraska 2023

Nebraska Travel Guide, Nebraska Tourism, 2024

Peck, David J. *Or Perish in the Attempt: The Hardship and Medicine of the Lewis and Clark Expedition*. The History Press, 2002

Plainsman Museum Walking Tour, Plainsman Museum

Rock Creek Station, Outdoor Nebraska, 2024

Rock Creek Station State Historical Park, Outdoor Nebraska, 2021

Rock Creek Station Walking Tour, Nebraska Game Parks

Rutter, Michael. *Bedside Book of Bad Girls: Outlaw Women of the American West*. Farcountry Press, 2008

Scott, Robert. *Plain Enemies: Best True Stories of the Frontier West*. Caxton Printers, 1995

Scotts Bluff Robidoux Pass, National Park Service

Wagner, Tricia Martineau. *It Happened on the Oregon Trail: Remarkable Events That Shaped History*. GPP, 2014

# Index

## Referenced by Sections

# B

Bates, General Delevan-see the Plainsman Museum

Bates House-see the Plainsman Museum

Battle of the Little Bighorn-see Fort Robinson

Beecher, Edith-see Homestead National Monument

Bidwell-Bartleson party-see Scott's Bluff

Black Hills-see Fort Robinson, Fort Hartsuff, Harold Warp's Pioneer Village

Bowman, Fay-see Harold Warp's Pioneer Village

Brando, Marlon-see Famous Nebraska Citizens

Brogan, James-see Fort Robinson

Buffett, Warren-see Famous Nebraska Citizens

Burdick, Gideon-see Scott's Bluff

Burlington Railroad-see Scott's Bluff

# C

California Trail-see Legacy of the Plains Museum

Campbell, William-see Gothenburg Pony Express Station

Carson, Johnny-see Famous Nebraska Citizens

Carson, Kit-see Rock Creek Station

## G

## H

## I

# About the Author

***Julie Bettendorf*** is a world traveler with a degree in archaeology and a background in history. She has traveled extensively throughout Egypt, Central America, South America, Europe, and the United Kingdom, visiting archaeological and historical sites all along the way.

Currently, Julie is traveling around the US visiting ghost towns, ancient rock art sites, and archaeological wonders as part of research for her ongoing historical travel series entitled ***Wandering Woman***. Wandering Woman is a set of state-by-state guides, full of photographs, historical anecdotes, and unique tips to help other women travel and explore solo across the US by car. Julie enjoys writing freelance blogs, traveling frequently with her two adult children, and hiking outdoors with her faithful dog companion Rosie.

# Also by Julie Bettendorf

***Wandering Woman: Nebraska*** is the most recent book in the ***Wandering Woman Travel Series***. The previous books ***Wandering Woman: Montana***, ***Colorado***, ***Utah***, ***Nevada***, ***Arizona***, ***Oregon***, ***Washington***, ***Idaho***, ***New Mexico***, ***Wyoming***, ***Northern California***, ***Southern California***, *and* ***Kansas*** are available in ebook and paperback.

Julie has published two children's books in an ongoing, beautifully illustrated travel series entitled ***Anthony Ant Goes to France*** and ***Anthony Ant Goes to Egypt***.

She has also published a work of historical fiction entitled ***Luxor: Book of Past Lives*** which has recently been released as an audiobook, read by renowned narrator Barry Shannon.